EVANGELINE

EVANGELINE

A Tale of Acadie
by

Henry Wadsworth Longfellow

NIMBUS
PUBLISHING

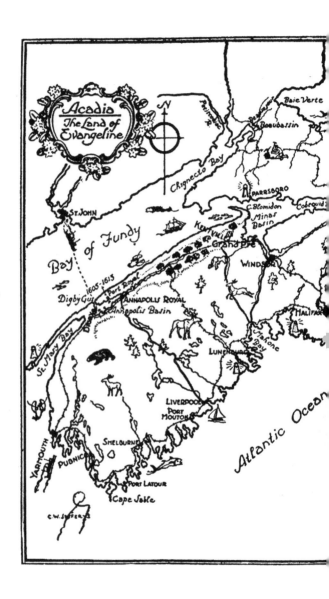

The Evangeline Country

Minas Basin

Blomidon

Longspell Point
Kingsport
Porter Pt.
Evangeline Beach
Boot Island
Long Island
Starr Pt.
Memorial Park
Grand Pré
Avonport
Wolfville
To Windsor
Melanson
Gaspereau R.
Gaspereau

Main Road
Secondary Road
Local Road
Railway

Nimbus Publishing Limited
PO Box 9166
Halifax, NS   B3K 5M8
(902) 455-4286
www.nimbus.ns.ca

National Library of Canada Cataloguing in Publication

   Longfellow, Henry Wadsworth, 1807-1882.
   Evangeline : a tale of Acadie / Henry Wadsworth
   Longfellow ; introduction by Sally Ross and
   Barbara LeBlanc.

   1-55109-468-1

1. Acadians—Expulsion, 1755—Poetry. I. Ross, Sally
II. Le Blanc, Barbara, 1951- III. Title.

PS2263.A1 2003a   811'.3   C2003-903507-7

Printed in Canada

The Genesis and Impact of *Evangeline*

Evangeline, A Tale of Acadie, the long romantic poem by Henry Wadsworth Longfellow, represents a milestone in the awakening of the collective consciousness of the Acadian people. Not only did Acadians identify with the story of Evangeline, but they saw their history acquire prestige and notoriety thanks to the international success of a work of fiction. By lifting Acadie out of the forgotten past, Longfellow honoured the courage and tenacity of the Acadian people.

How did an American poet who had never visited Nova Scotia become interested in the tragic story of the deportation (1755-1763) of the Acadians? Why did his epic poem capture the imagination of readers all over the world? Why did this poem have such a profound impact on the Acadian people?

⚜ ⚜ ⚜

Henry Wadsworth Longfellow was born on February 27, 1807, in Portland, Maine. He spent most of his youth in this quiet and charming town that inspired a number of his poems. When he was a young adolescent, he left for Bourdoin College, located about thirty miles from Portland. One of his classmates was Nathaniel Hawthorne, the future novelist who was to play a major role in the genesis of *Evangeline*.

After he graduated, Longfellow spent three years in Europe. He returned to the United States in 1829 to take a position at his alma mater, where he taught literarture for several years. In 1835, he and his wife decided to tour Europe. In the course of their travels, his wife took sick and died in Rotterdam. In 1836, Longfellow accepted a position as professor of modern languages at Harvard University in Cambridge, Massachusetts. During the seventeen years that he taught at Harvard, he continued to write poetry and translated a number of French and Spanish literary works.

In 1842, he left once again for Europe and remarried after he returned to

Massachusetts. Several years after the publication of *Evangeline, A Tale of Acadie* in 1847, he resigned from his position at Harvard in order to devote himself exclusively to writing. The 1860s left Longfellow shattered by the events of the Civil War, the tragic death of his second wife and the death of his great friend Nathaniel Hawthorne. After another trip to Europe, where he was received with full honours, he returned to Cambridge where he spent the last twenty years of his life surrounded by friends. He died on May 24, 1882.

In order to understand the impact and cultural significance of the poem *Evangeline*, one should be aware of the historical events that led up to the deportation of the Acadians. Founded in 1604, but settled only after 1632, the French colony of Acadie covered the strategic territory that lay between New France (Quebec) and New England.

Unlike the huge French colony of New France, Acadie did not benefit from a French regime that flourished without interruption from 1608 to 1760. Not only did Acadie change hands on numerous occasions, but it was captured in 1710, fifty years before the fall of New France. According to the Treaty of Utrecht, signed in 1713 between France and Great Britain, France lost Acadie and Newfoundland, but kept Isle Royale (Cape Breton Island) and Isle Saint Jean (Prince Edward Island). The Acadians, who were Catholic and French-speaking, now found themselves in a Protestant and British colony that had been renamed Nova Scotia.

Under the terms of the Treaty of Utrecht, the Acadians were given a year to sign an oath of allegiance to the British monarch or to leave their fertile farms and settle on the French colony of Isle Royale. They refused to swear an unconditional oath of loyalty because they wanted to be guaranteed religious freedom and to be exempt from taking up arms against either the French or the Mi'kmaq in the event of war. After years of negotiations, the governor of Nova Scotia appeared to accept these conditions since the Acadians became known as the Neutrals or French Neutrals. The British authorities succeeded in convincing the majority of Acadian men to sign the oath of allegiance by promising them that they would not have to bear arms. In some cases, this promise was written in the margin of the French translation of the oath, and in other cases it was merely a verbal assurance.

Aside from the question of the oath of allegiance, the Acadians enjoyed a period of relative peace and prosperity that lasted until the late 1740s—a period which some historians call the Golden Age of Acadie. War broke out once again between France and Great Britain in 1744. As a result, tensions grew in the colonies. The British built a fort in Piziquid (Windsor) and another one overlooking the marshes of Beaubassin (near the border of present-day New Brunswick and Nova Scotia). The following year, France countered by constructing Fort Beauséjour and Fort Gaspareau. The founding of Halifax in 1749 had also marked a turning point in the development of the colony of Nova Scotia. On the one hand, it established a solid British presence on the Atlantic coast midway between Boston and the large French fortress at Louisbourg on Isle Royale (Cape

Breton Island). On the other hand, it constituted the first step in a systematic effort to colonize Nova Scotia with Protestant settlers who would eventually outnumber the French-speaking and Catholic Acadians.

In 1754, Charles Lawrence became lieutenant-governor of Nova Scotia. Like Governor William Shirley of Massachusetts, he had become increasingly suspicious of the Acadians' neutrality. Consequently he decided to take more aggressive measures. With the reinforcement of 2,000 volunteer troops from Massachusetts, Lieutenant-Colonel Robert Monckton captured the French forts at Beauséjour and Gaspareau.

Shortly after the fall of Fort Beauséjour, Captain Alexander Murray, who was stationed at Fort Edward in Piziquid, confiscated the guns and ammunition of the Acadians living in Grand-Pré, the most populated Acadian settlement. In July 1755, Lawrence ordered representatives of the various Acadian settlements to appear before the Council in Halifax in order to sign the unconditional oath of allegiance to the British Monarch. The delegates refused to sign the oath before consulting the inhabitants of their respective villages. As a result, they were imprisoned on George's Island in Halifax Harbour. On July 28, 1755, the Council in Halifax decided to proceed with the removal of the "French inhabitants" from the colony of Nova Scotia.

Although Grand-Pré has become the symbol of the expulsion of the Acadians, the deportation actually began at Fort Beauséjour (renamed Fort Cumberland) in August 1755. The inhabitants in the area were rounded up and imprisoned in the fort prior to being shipped to the British colonies along the eastern seaboard.

One month later, the deportation of the Acadians began at Grand-Pré. On September 5, Lieutenant-Colonel John Winslow, commander of the New England regiment stationed in the area, ordered the male inhabitants to assemble in the church Saint Charles des Mines. In other villages, the Acadians were informed that their lands, their houses and their livestock would be confiscated and that they and their families would be transported out of Nova Scotia. It is estimated that approximately 6,000 Acadians were deported from mainland Nova Scotia in 1755.

Although many Acadians perished on board the transport ships, the survivors were distributed in allotments to Massachusetts, Connecticut, New York, Pennsylvania, Maryland, Virginia, North Carolina, South Carolina and Georgia. Contrary to popular belief, no Acadians were actually deported from Nova Scotia to Louisiana since it was not a British colony.

After the fall of Louisbourg in 1758, the majority of Acadians living on Isle Royale and Isle Saint Jean were deported to England or France. Over a period of several years, the entire French-speaking population of the Atlantic region was thus shattered and dispersed. For the majority of the estimated 10,000 Acadians it meant deportation and life in exile, for others it meant a few years in hiding and for others almost fifty years of wandering.

In 1764, Acadians were given permission to resettle in Nova Scotia provided they took the oath of allegiance and settled in small groups in distant parts of the colony. As one

of the darkest chapters in the history of Nova
Scotia came to an end, the slow reconstruc-
tion of a people began.

When Henry Wadsworth Longfellow
wrote his famous poem, there were only two
historical works that described the deporta-
tion of the Acadians. One, published in 1770,
was by Abbé Guillaume Raynal and the
other, published in 1829, was by Thomas
Chandler Haliburton. It is known that
Longfellow borrowed a copy of Haliburton's
book, *History of Nova Scotia*, from the library
at Harvard on March 1841 and that he con-
sulted *L'histoire philosophique et politique du
commerce et des établissements des Européens dans
les deux Indes* by Raynal. It was prior to that,
however, that he was inspired to write a
poem on the fate of the Acadians. Rev.
Horace Lorenzo Conolly, an Anglican priest
and friend of Nathaniel Hawthorne, had told
him about two newlyweds who were separated
by the deportation and how the young
woman had wandered for years in search of
her lover. She eventually found him, but he
was on his death bed. The priest said a

French-Canadian told him this tragic story about the young couple from Acadie. After listening to the story, Longfellow is reported to have said: "It is the best illustration of faithfulness and the constancy of a woman that I have ever heard or read." In 1845, he began writing his poetic version of the story. It was published two years later. Translated into many different languages, *Evangeline, A Tale of Acadie*, became an international best-seller.

The first edition of Pamphile Lemay's French translation of *Evangeline* was published in 1865 and, two years later, it appeared in serial form in the newspaper *Le Moniteur acadien*. In 1887, *L'Évangéline*, an Acadian newspaper named after Longfellow's heroine, also published the poem. By 1907, Acadian schoolchildren throughout the Maritime Provinces were reading extracts of the poem featured in one of their readers.

In the first part of the poem, Longfellow tells the story of two lovers, Gabriel Lajeunesse and Evangeline Bellefontaine, who grew up together in the beautiful village of Grand-Pré. Everything is perfect in this land of peace and plenty, an earthly paradise where pious Acadians work together in harmony. The engagement ceremony of the young lovers takes place under the watchful eye of the notary, René LeBlanc, and their fathers, Benedict and Basil. The following day, the engagement party is suddenly interrupted by the arrival of British soldiers and the sound of drums. The men and boys of the village are rounded up in the church where the commanding officer reads the order of deportation and informs them that their land, houses and livestock have been confiscated. Loaded onto British transport ships, the habitants of Grand-Pré watch as a wall of fire consumes their village. Evangeline and Gabriel are separated and their idyllic life comes to an end.

In the second part of the poem, we follow Evangeline as she wanders the continent in search of her beloved Gabriel. Her hope of finding him is renewed each time she encounters other exiled Acadians who assure her that he is not far off. She just misses him in the bayous of Louisiana. After years of wandering, Evangeline settles in Philadelphia where she works as a Sister of Mercy tending the sick and the poor. One day, in the middle of a smallpox epidemic, Evangeline finds Gabriel on his death bed in a hospital. He dies in her arms and shortly after, broken-hearted, she follows her fiancé to the grave.

Evangeline symbolizes loyalty, courage, piety and patience. These were important qualities for the Acadian nationalists of the late nineteenth century who were attempting to unite Acadians scattered throughout Nova Scotia, New Brunswick and Prince Edward Island. Evangeline became a figurehead and source of inspiration that reinforced the feeling of belonging to a people. A similar phenomenon took place in Louisiana, where Evangeline also served to link Acadians of the south to Acadians of the north. In 1930, for example, Senator Dudley LeBlanc led a delegation of Evangelines to Canada. These young women visited various Acadian communities in Quebec, New Brunswick and Nova Scotia. Evangeline, the fictitious young woman from Grand-Pré immortalized by Longfellow, captured the imagination of Acadians for several generations.

After the construction of the railway in southeastern Nova Scotia in the 1870s, *Evangeline* also helped promote tourism. Thanks to the beauty of Longfellow's poetry and his emotionally appealing heroine, thousands of American tourists travelled to Nova Scotia looking for the "Land of Evangeline." In 1907, John Frederick Herbin, whose mother, Marie Robichaud, was an Acadian, bought an historically significant piece of land in Grand-Pré with the idea of developing a commemorative park dedicated to the memory of the Acadians. Ten years later, he sold the property to the Dominion Atlantic Railway, which erected the famous statue of Evangeline by the sculptors Philippe and Henri Hébert from Quebec. The Grand-Pré commemorative park became a national historic site in 1961.

Evangeline is a superb example of romantic poetry and a masterpiece of world literature. Longfellow was not the first author to provide an historical setting for a poignant love story. However, he brought the tragedy of the deportation of the Acadians to the attention of readers all over the world. Longfellow gave the Acadians an icon whose constancy in love and adversity still captivates our imagination.

Sally Ross & Barbara LeBlanc

References

Candow, James E. "The Deportation of the Acadians," booklet published by Environment Canada, Parks, 1986.

Fergusson, C. Bruce. "Introduction to *Evangeline, A Tale of Acadie.*" *Evangeline.* Halifax: Nimbus Publishing Limited, 1951.

Griffiths, Naomi. "Longfellow's *Evangeline*: The Birth and Acceptance of a Legend." *Acadiensis.* Spring: 1982.

LeBlanc, Barbara. "*Evangeline* as Identity Myth." *Journal of the Canadian Association of Ethnology and Folklore.* Vol. 15, No. 2: 1993.

Maillet, Marguerite. *Histoire de la littérature acadienne.* Moncton: Éditions d'Acadie, 1983.

Pellerin, Ginette. *Evangeline's Quest.* National Film Board of Canada, 1996.

Ross, Sally and J. Alphonse Deveau. *The Acadians of Nova Scotia.* Halifax: Nimbus Publishing, 1992.

Thériault, Léon. "Historical Synthesis, 1763-1990," in Jean Daigle, ed., *Acadia of the Maritimes.* Chaire d'études acadiennes: Université de Moncton, 1995.

Evangeline

A Tale of Acadie

THIS is the forest primeval. The murmuring pines
and the hemlocks,
Bearded with moss, and in garments green, indistinct in
the twilight,
Stand like Druids of eld, with voices sad and prophetic,
Stand like harpers hoar, with beards that rest on their
bosoms.
Loud from its rocky caverns, the deep-voiced
neighbouring ocean
Speaks, and in accents disconsolate answers the wail of
the forest.

This is the forest primeval; but where are the hearts
that beneath it
Leaped like the roe, when he hears in the woodland the
voice of the huntsman?
Where is the thatch-roofed village, the home of
Acadian farmers,—
Men whose lives glided on like rivers that water the
woodlands,

Darkened by shadows of earth, but reflecting an image
 of heaven?
Waste are those pleasant farms, and the farmers for ever
 departed!
Scattered like dust and leaves, when the mighty blasts
 of October
Seize them, and whirl them aloft, and sprinkle them far
 o'er the ocean.
Naught but tradition remains of the beautiful village of
 Grand-Pré.
Ye who believe in affection that hopes, and endures,
 and is patient,
Ye who believe in the beauty and strength of woman's
 devotion,
List to the mournful tradition, still sung by the pines of
 the forest;
List to a Tale of Love in Acadie, home of the happy.

PART THE FIRST

I

IN the Acadian land, on the shores of the Basin of
 Minas,
Distant, secluded, still, the little village of Grand-Pré
Lay in the fruitful valley. Vast meadows stretched to the
 eastward,
Giving the village its name, and pasture to flocks
 without number.
Dikes, that the hands of the farmers had raised with
 labour incessant,
Shut out the turbulent tides; but at stated seasons the
 flood-gates
Opened, and welcomed the sea to wander at will o'er
 the meadows.
West and south there were fields of flax, and orchards
 and cornfields

Spreading afar and unfenced o'er the plain; and away to
  the northward
Blomidon rose, and the forests old, and aloft on the
  mountains
Sea-fogs pitched their tents, and mists from the mighty
  Atlantic
Looked on the happy valley, but ne'er from their station
  descended.
There, in the midst of its farms, reposed the Acadian
  village.
Strongly built were the houses, with frames of oak and
  of hemlock,
Such as the peasants of Normandy built in the reign of
  the Henries.
Thatched were the roofs, with dormer-windows; and
  gables projecting
Over the basement below protected and shaded the
  door-way.
There in the tranquil evenings of summer, when
  brightly the sunset
Lighted the village street, and gilded the vanes on the
  chimneys,
Matrons and maidens sat in snow-white caps and in
  kirtles
Scarlet and blue and green, with distaffs spinning the
  golden
Flax for the gossiping looms, whose noisy shuttles
  within doors
Mingled their sound with the whir of the wheels and the
  songs of the maidens.
Solemnly down the street came the parish priest, and
  the children
Paused in their play to kiss the hand he extended to
  bless them.
Reverend walked he among them; and up rose matrons
  and maidens,
Hailing his slow approach with words of affectionate
  welcome.

Then came the labourers home from the field, and
    serenely the sun sank
Down to his rest, and twilight prevailed. Anon from the
    belfry
Softly the Angelus sounded, and over the roofs of the
    village
Columns of pale blue smoke, like clouds of incense
    ascending,
Rose from a hundred hearths, the homes of peace and
    contentment.
Thus dwelt together in love these simple Acadian
    farmers,—
Dwelt in the love of God and of man. Alike were they
    free from
Fear, that reigns with the tyrant, and envy, the vice of
    republics.
Neither locks had they to their doors, nor bars to their
    windows;
But their dwellings were open as day and the hearts of
    the owners;
Their the richest was poor, and the poorest lived in
    abundance.

  Somewhat apart from the village, and nearer the
    Basin of Minas,
Benedict Bellefontaine, the wealthiest farmer of Grand-
    Pré,
Dwelt on his goodly acres; and with him, directing his
    household,
Gentle Evangeline lived, his child, and the pride of the
    village.
Stalworth and stately in form was the man of seventy
    winters;
Hearty and hale was he, an oak that is covered with
    snowflakes;
White as the snow were his locks, and his cheeks as
    brown as the oak-leaves.

Fair was she to behold, that maiden of seventeen
summers.
Black were her eyes as the berry that grows on the thorn
by the way-side,
Black, yet how softly they gleamed beneath the brown
shade of her tresses!
Sweet was her breath as the breath of kine that feed in
the meadows.
When in the harvest heat she bore to the reapers at
noontide
Flagons of home-brewed ale, ah! fair in sooth was the
maiden.
Fairer was she when, on Sunday morn, while the bell
from its turret
Sprinkled with holy sounds the air, as the priest with his
hyssop
Sprinkles the congregation, and scatters blessings upon
them,
Down the long street she passed, with her chaplet of
beads and her missal,
Wearing her Norman cap, and her kirtle of blue, and
the ear-rings,
Brought in the olden time from France, and since, as an
heirloom,
Handed down from mother to child, through long
generations.
But a celestial brightness — a more ethereal beauty—
Shone on her face and encircled her form, when, after
confession,
Homeward serenely she walked with God's benediction
upon her.
When she had passed, it seemed like the ceasing of
exquisite music.

Firmly builded with rafters of oak, the house of the
farmer

Stood on the side of a hill commanding the sea; and a shady
Sycamore grew by the door, with a woodbine wreathing around it.
Rudely carved was the porch, with seats beneath; and a footpath
Led through an orchard wide, and disappeared in the meadow.
Under the sycamore-tree were hives overhung by a penthouse,
Such as the traveller sees in regions remote by the road-side,
Built o'er a box for the poor, or the blessed image of Mary.
Farther down, on the slope of the hill, was the well with its moss-grown
Bucket, fastened with iron, and near it a trough for the horses.
Shielding the house from storms, on the north, were the barns and the farm-yard.
There stood the broad-wheeled wains and the antique ploughs and the harrows;
There were the folds for the sheep; and there, in his feathered seraglio,
Strutted the lordly turkey, and crowed the cock, with the self-same
Voice that in ages of old had startled the penitent Peter.
Bursting with hay were the barns, themselves a village. In each one
Far o'er the gable projected a roof of thatch; and a staircase,
Under the sheltering eaves, led up to the odorous corn-loft.
There too the dove-cot stood, with its meek and innocent inmates
Murmuring ever of love; while above in the variant breezes

Numberless noisy weathercocks rattled and sang of
    mutation.

   Thus, at peace with God and the world, the farmer of
       Grand-Pré
Lived on his sunny farm, and Evangeline governed his
    household.
Many a youth, as he knelt in church and opened his
    missal,
Fixed his eyes upon her as the saint of his deepest
    devotion;
Happy was he who might touch her hand or the hem of
    her garment!
Many a suitor came to her door, by the darkness
    befriended,
And, as he knocked and waited to hear the sound of her
    footsteps,
Knew not which beat the louder, his heart or the
    knocker of iron;
Or at the joyous feast of the Patron Saint of the village,
Bolder grew, and pressed her hand in the dance as he
    whispered
Hurried words of love, that seemed a part of the music.
But, among all who came, young Gabriel only was
    welcome;
Gabriel Lajuenesse, the son of Basil the blacksmith,
Who was a mighty man in the village, and honoured of
    all men;
For, since the birth of time, throughout all ages and
    nations,
Has the craft of the smith been held in repute by the
    people.
Basil was Benedict's friend. Their children from earliest
    childhood
Grew up together as brother and sister; and Father
    Felician,

Priest and pedagogue both in the village, had taught
them their letters

Out of the self-same book, with the hymns of the
church and the plain-song.

But when the hymn was sung, and the daily lesson
completed,

Swiftly they hurried away to the forge of Basil the
blacksmith.

There at the door they stood, with wondering eyes to
behold him

Take in his leathern lap the hoof of the horse as a
plaything.

Nailing the shoe in its place; while near him the tire of
the cart-wheel

Lay like a fiery snake, coiled round in a cirle of cinders

Oft on autumnal eves, when without in the gathering
darkness

Bursting with light seemed the smithy, through every
cranny and crevice,

Warm by the forge within they watched the labouring
bellows,

And as its panting ceased, and the sparks expired in the
ashes,

Merrily laughed, and said they were nuns going into the
chapel.

Oft on sledges in winter, as swift as the swoop of the
eagle,

Down the hillside bounding, they glided away o'er the
meadow.

Oft in the barns they climbed to the populous nests on
the rafters,

Seeking with eager eyes that wondrous stone, which the
swallow

Brings from the shore of the sea to restore the sight of its
fledglings;

Lucky was he who found that stone in the nest of the
swallow!

Thus passed a few swift years, and they no longer were
    children.
He was a valiant youth, and his face, like the face of the
    morning,
Gladdened the earth with its light, and ripened thought
    into action.
She was a woman now, with the heart and hopes of a
    woman.
"Sunshine of Saint Eulalie" was she called; for that was
    the sunshine
Which, as the farmers believed, would load their
    orchards with apples;
She, too, would bring to her husband's house delight
    and abundance,
Filling it with love and the ruddy faces of children.

II

Now had the season returned, when the nights grow
    colder and longer,
And the retreating sun the sign of the Scorpion enters.
Birds of passage sailed through the leaden air, from the
    ice-bound,
Desolate northern bays to the shores of tropical islands.
Harvests were gathered in; and wild with the winds of
    September
Wrestled the trees of the forest, as Jacob of old with the
    angel.
All the signs foretold a winter long and inclement.
Bees, with prophetic instinct of want, had hoarded their
    honey
Till the hives overflowed; and the Indian hunters
    asserted
Cold would the winter be, for thick was the fur of the
    foxes.
Such was the advent of autumn. Then followed that
    beautiful season,

Called by the pious Acadian peasants the Summer of
All-Saints!
Filled was the air with a dreamy and magical light; and
the landscape
Lay as if new-created in all the freshness of childhood.
Peace seemed to reign upon earth, and the restless heart
of the ocean
Was for a moment consoled. All sounds were in
harmony blended.
Voices of children at play, the crowing of cocks in the
farm-yards,
Whir of wings in the drowsy air, and the cooing of
pigeons,
All were subdued and low as the murmurs of love, and
the great sun
Looked with the eye of love through the golden vapours
around him;
While arrayed in its robes of russet and scarlet and
yellow,
Bright with the sheen of the dew, each glittering tree of
the forest
Flashed like the plane-tree the Persian adorned with
mantles and jewels.

Now recommenced the reign of rest and affection
and stillness.
Day with its burden and heat had departed, and
twilight descending
Brought back the evening star to the sky, and the herds
to the homestead.
Pawing the ground they came, and resting their necks
on each other,
And with their nostrils distended inhaling the freshness
of evening.
Foremost, bearing the bell, Evangeline's beautiful
heifer,

Proud of her snow-white hide, and the ribbon that
    waved from her collar,
Quietly paced and slow, as if conscious of human
    affection.
Then came the shepherd back with his bleating flocks
    from the sea-side,
Where was their favorite pasture. Behind them
    followed the watch-dog,
Patient, full of importance, and gained in the pride of
    his instinct,
Walking from side to side with a lordly air, and
    superbly
Waving his bushy tail, and urging forward the
    stragglers;
Regent of flocks was he when the shepherd slept; their
    protector,
When from the forest at night through the starry
    silence, the wolves howled.
Late, with the rising moon, returned the wains from the
    marshes,
Laden with briny hay, that filled the air with its odour.
Cheerily neighed the steeds, with dew on their manes
    and their fetlocks,
While aloft on their shoulders the wooden and
    ponderous saddles,
Painted with brilliant dyes, and adorned with tassels of
    crimson,
Nodded in bright array, like hollyhocks heavy with
    blossoms.
Patiently stood the cows meanwhile, and yielded their
    udders
Unto the milkmaid's hand; whilst loud and in regular
    cadence
Into the sounding pails the foaming streamlets
    descended.
Lowing of cattle and peals of laughter were heard in the
    farm-yard,

Echoed back by the barns. Anon they sank into
    stillness;
Heavily closed, with a jarring sound, the valves of the
    barn-doors,
Rattled the wooden bars, and all for a season was silent.

Indoors, warm by the wide-mouthed fireplace, idly
    the farmer
Sat in his elbow-chair, and watched how the flames and
    the smoke-wreaths
Struggled together like foes in a burning city. Behind
    him,
Nodding and mocking along the wall, with gestures
    fantastic,
Darted his own huge shadow, and vanished away into
    darkness.
Faces, clumsily carved in oak, on the back of his arm-
    chair
Laughed in the flickering light; and the pewter plates on
    the dresser
Caught and reflected the flame, as shields of armies the
    sunshine.
Fragments of song the old man sang, and carols of
    Christmas,
Such as at home, in the olden time, his fathers before
    him
Sang in their Norman orchards and bright Burgundian
    vineyards.
Close at her father's side was the gentle Evangeline
    seated,
Spinning flax for the loom, that stood in the corner
    behind her.
Silent awhile were its treadles, at rest was its diligent
    shuttle,
While the monotonous drone of the wheel, like the
    drone of a bagpipe,

Followed the old man's song and united the fragments
together.
As in a church, when the chant of the choir at intervals
ceases,
Footfalls are heard in the aisles, or words of the priest at
the altar,
So, in each pause of the song, with measured motion
the clock clicked.

Thus, as they sat, there were footsteps heard, and,
suddenly lifted,
Sounded the wooden latch, and the door swung back
on its hinges.
Benedict knew by the hob-nailed shoes it was Basil the
blacksmith,
And by her beating heart Evangeline knew who was
with him.
"Welcome!" the farmer exclaimed, as their footsteps
paused on the threshold,
"Welcome, Basil, my friend! Come, take thy place on
the settle
Close by the chimney-side, which is always empty
without thee;
Take from the shelf overhead thy pipe and the box of
tobacco;
Never so much thyself art thou as when through the
curling
Smoke of the pipe or the forge thy friendly and jovial
face gleams
Round and red as the harvest moon through the midst
of the marshes."
Then, with a smile of content, thus answered Basil the
blacksmith,
Taking with easy air the accustomed seat by the
fireside:—
"Benedict Bellefontaine, thou hast ever thy jest and thy
ballad!

Ever in the cheerfullest mood art thou, when others are
   filled with
Gloomy forebodings of ill, and see only ruin before
   them.
Happy art thou, as if every day thou hadst picked up a
   horseshoe."
Pausing a moment, to take the pipe that Evangeline
   brought him,
And with a coal from the embers had lighted, he slowly
   continued:—
"Four days now are passed since the English ships at
   their anchors
Ride in the Gaspereau's mouth, with their cannon
   pointed against us.
What their design may be is unknown; but all are
   commanded
On the morrow to meet in the church, where his
   Majesty's mandate
Will be proclaimed as law in the land. Alas! in the
   meantime
Many surmises of evil alarm the hearts of the people."
Then made answer the farmer:— "Perhaps some
   friendlier purpose
Brings these ships to our shores. Perhaps the harvests in
   England
By untimely rains or untimlier heat have been blighted,
And from our bursting barns they would feed their
   cattle and children."
"Not so thinketh the folk in the village," said, warmly,
   the blacksmith,
Shaking his head, as in doubt; then, heaving a sigh, he
   continued:—
"Louisbourg is not forgotten, nor Beau Séjour, nor Port
   Royal.
Many already have fled to the forest, and lurk on its
   outskirts.
Waiting with anxious hearts the dubious fate of to-
   morrow.

Arms have been taken from us, and warlike weapons of
    all kinds;
Nothing is left but the blacksmith's sledge and the
    scythe of the mower."
Then with a pleasant smile made answer the jovial
    farmer:—
"Safer are we unarmed, in the midst of our flocks and
    our cornfields,
Safer within these peaceful dikes, beseiged by the
    ocean,
Than our fathers in forts, beseiged by the enemy's
    cannon.
Fear no evil, my friend, and to-night may no shadow of
    sorrow
Fall on this house and hearth; for this is the night of the
    contract.
Built are the house and barn. The merry lads of the
    village
Strongly have built them and well; and, breaking the
    glebe round about them,
Filled the barn with hay, and the house with food for a
    twelvemonth.
René Leblanc will be here anon, with his papers and
    inkhorn.
Shall we not then be glad, and rejoice in the joy of our
    children?"
As apart by the window she stood, with her hand in her
    lover's,
Blushing Evangeline heard the words that her father
    had spoken,
And, as they died on his lips, the worthy notary entered.

III

Bent like a laboring oar, that toils in the surf of the
    ocean,

Bent, but not broken, by age was the form of the notary
    public;
Shocks of yellow hair, like the silken floss of the maize,
    hung
Over his shoulders; his forehead was high; and glasses
    with horn bows
Sat astride on his nose, with a look of wisdom supernal.
Father of twenty children was he, and more than a
    hundred
Children's children rode on his knee, and heard his
    great watch tick.
Four long years in the times of the war had he
    languished a captive,
Suffering much in an old French fort as the friend of the
    English.
Now, though warier grown, without all guile or
    suspicion,
Ripe in wisdom was he, but patient, and simple, and
    childlike.
He was beloved by all, and most of all by the children;
For he told them tales of the Loup-garou in the forest,
And of the goblin that came in the night to water the
    horses,
And of the white Létiche, the ghost of a child who
    unchristened
Died, and was doomed to haunt unseen the chambers of
    children;
And how on Christmas eve the oxen talked in the
    stable,
And how the fever was cured by a spider shut up in a
    nutshell,
And of the marvellous powers of four-leaved clover and
    horseshoes,
With whatsoever else was writ in the lore of the village.
Then up rose from his seat by the fireside Basil the
    blacksmith,
Knocked from his pipe the ashes, and slowly extending
    his right hand,

"Father LeBlanc," he exclaimed, "thou hast heard the
talk in the village,
And perchance, canst tell us some news of these ships
and their errand."
Then with modest demeanour made answer the notary
public,
"Gossip enough have I heard, in sooth, yet am never the
wiser;
And what their errand may be I know not better than
others.
Yet am I not of those who imagine some evil intention
Brings them here, for we are at peace; and why then
molest us?"
"God's name!" shouted the hasty and somewhat
irascible blacksmith;
"Must we in all things look for the how, and the why,
and the wherefore?
Daily injustice is done, and might is the right of the
strongest!"
But without heeding his warmth, continued the notary
public—
"Man is unjust, but God is just; and finally justice
Triumphs; and well I remember a story, that often
consoled me,
When as a captive I lay in the old French fort at Port
Royal."
This was the old man's favorite tale, and he loved to
repeat it
When his neighbours complained that any injustice was
done them.
"Once in an ancient city, whose name I no longer
remember,
Raised aloft on a column, a brazen statue of Justice
Stood in the public square, upholding the scales in its
left hand,
And in its right a sword, as an emblem that justice
presided

Over the laws of the land, and the hearts and homes of
    the people.
Even the birds had built their nests in the scales of the
    balance,
Having no fear of the sword that flashed in the sunshine
    above them.
But in the course of time the laws of the land were
    corrupted;
Might took the place of right, and the weak were
    oppressed, and the mighty
Ruled with an iron rod. Then it chanced in a
    nobleman's palace
That a necklace of pearls was lost, and ere long a
    suspicion
Fell on an orphan girl who lived as a maid in the
    household.
She, after form of trial, condemned to die on the
    scaffold,
Patiently met her doom at the foot of the statue of
    Justice.
As to her Father in Heaven her innocent spirit
    ascended,
Lo! o'er the city a tempest rose; and the bolts of the
    thunder
Smote the statue of bronze, and hurled in wrath from its
    left hand
Down on the pavement below the clattering scales of
    the balance,
And in the hollow thereof was found the nest of a
    magpie,
Into whose clay-built walls the necklace of pearls was
    inwoven."
Silenced, but not convinced, when the story was ended,
    the blacksmith
Stood like a man who fain would speak, but findeth no
    language;

All his thoughts were congealed into lines on his face,
    as the vapours
Freeze in fantastic shapes on the window-panes in the
    winter.

    Then Evangeline lighted the brazen lamp on the
    table,
Filled, till it overflowed, the pewter tankard with
    home-brewed
Nut-brown ale, that was famed for its strength in the
    village of Grand-Pré;
While from his pocket the notary drew his papers and
    inkhorn,
Wrote with a steady hand the date and the age of the
    parties,
Naming the dower of the bride in flocks of sheep and in
    cattle.
Orderly all things proceeded, and duly and well were
    completed,
And the great seal of the law was set like a sun on the
    margin.
Then from his leathern pouch the farmer threw on the
    table
Three times the old man's fee in solid pieces of silver;
And the notary rising, and blessing the bride and the
    bridegroom,
Lifted aloft the tankard of ale and drank to their
    welfare.
Wiping the foam from his lip, he solemnly bowed and
    departed,
While in silence the others sat and mused by the
    fireside,
Till Evangeline brought the draughtboard out of its
    corner.
Soon was the game begun. In friendly contention the
    old men

Laughed at each lucky hit, or unsuccessful manoeuvre,
Laughed when a man was crowned, or a breach was
    made in the king-row.
Meanwhile, apart, in the twilight gloom of a window's
    embrasure,
Sat the lovers, and whispered together, beholding the
    moon rise
Over the pallid sea and the silvery mist of the meadows.
Silently one by one, in the infinite meadows of heaven,
Blossomed the lovely stars, the forget-me-nots of the
    angels.

Thus was the evening passed. Anon the bell from the
    belfry
Rang out the hour of nine, the village curfew, and
    straightway
Rose the guests and departed; and silence reigned in the
    household.
Many a farewell word and sweet goodnight on the
    doorstep
Lingered long in Evangeline's heart, and filled it with
    gladness.
Carefully then were covered the embers that glowed on
    the hearth-stone,
And on the oaken stairs resounded the tread of the
    farmer.
Soon with a soundless step the foot of Evangeline
    followed.
Up the staircase moved a luminous space in the
    darkness,
Lighted less by lamp than the shining face of the
    maiden.
Silent she passed the hall, and entered the door of her
    chamber.
Simple that chamber was, with its curtains of white,
    and its clothespress

Ample and high, on whose spacious shelves were carefully folded

Linen and woollen tuffs, by the hand of Evangeline woven.

This was the precious dower she would bring to her husband in marriage,

Better than flocks and herds, being proofs of her skill as a housewife.

Soon she extinguished her lamp, for the mellow and radiant moonlight

Streamed through the windows, and lighted the room, till the heart of the maiden

Swelled and obeyed its power, like the tremulous tides of the ocean.

Ah! she was fair, exceeding fair to behold, as she stood with

Naked snow-white feet on the gleaming floor of her chamber!

Little she dreamed that below, among the trees of the orchard,

Waited her lover and watched for the gleam of her lamp and her shadow.

Yet were her thoughts of him, and at times a feeling of sadness

Passed o'er her soul, as the sailing shade of clouds in the moonlight

Flitted across the floor and darkened the room for a moment.

And, as she gazed from the window, she saw serenely the moon pass.

Forth from the folds of a cloud, and one star follow her footsteps,

As out of Abraham's tent young Ishmael wandered with Hagar!

IV

Pleasantly rose next morn the sun on the village of Grand-Pré.

Pleasantly gleamed in the soft, sweet air the Basin of Minas,

Where the ships, with their wavering shadows, were riding at anchor.

Life had long been astir in the village, and clamorous labor

Knocked with its hundred hands at the golden gates of the morning.

Now from the country around, from the farms and neighboring hamlets,

Came in their holiday dresses the blithe Acadian peasants.

Many a glad good-morrow and jocund laugh from the young folk

Made the bright air brighter, as up from the numerous meadows,

Where no path could be seen but the track of wheels in the greenward,

Group after group appeared, and jointed, or passing on the highway.

Long ere noon, in the village all sounds of labour were silenced.

Thronged were the streets with people; and noisy groups at the house-doors

Sat in the cheerful sun, and rejoiced and gossiped together.

Every house was an inn, where all were welcomed and feasted;

For with this simple people, who lived like brothers together,

All things were held in common, and what one had was another's.

Yet under Benedict's roof hospitality seemed more abundant:

For Evangeline stood among the guests of her father;
Bright was her face with smiles, and words of welcome
and gladness
Fell from her beautiful lips, and blessed the cup as she
gave it.
Under the open sky, in the odorous air of the orchard,
Stript of its golden fruit, was spread the feast of
betrothal.
There in the shade of the porch were the priest and the
notary seated;
There good Benedict sat, and sturdy Basil the
blacksmith.
Not far withdrawn from these, by the cider-press and
the beehives,
Michael the fiddler was placed, with the gayest of
hearts and of waistcoats.
Shadow and light from the leaves alternately played on
his snow-white
Hair, as it waved in the wind; and the jolly face of the
fiddler
Glowed like a living coal when the ashes are blown
from the embers.
Gaily the old man sang to the vibrant sound of his
fiddle,
"Tous les Bourgeois de Chartres," and *"Le Carillon de
Dunkerque."*
And anon with his wooden shoes beat time to the
music.
Merrily, merrily whirled the wheels of the dizzying
dances
Under the orchard-trees and down the path to the
meadows;
Old folk and young together, and children mingled
among them.
Fairest of all the maids was Evangeline, Benedict's
daughter!
Noblest of all the youths was Gabriel, son of the
blacksmith!

So passed the morning away. And lo! with a
   summons sonorous
Sounded the bell from its tower, and over the meadows
   a drum beat.
Thronged ere long was the church with men. Without,
   in the churchyard,
Waited the women. They stood by the graves, and hung
   on the head-stones
Garlands of autumn-leaves and evergreens fresh from
   the forest.
Then came the guard from the ships, and marching
   proudly among them
Entered the sacred portal. With loud and dissonant
   clangour
Echoed the sound of their brazen drums from ceiling
   and casement,—
Echoed a moment only, and slowly the ponderous
   portal
Closed, and in silence the crowd awaited the will of the
   soldiers.
Then uprose their commander, and spake from the
   steps of the altar,
Holding aloft in his hands, with its seals, the royal
   commission.
"You are convened this day," he said, "by his Majesty's
   orders.
Clement and kind has he been; but how you have
   answered his kindness,
Let your own hearts reply! To my natural make and my
   temper
Painful the task is I do, which to you I know must be
   grievous.
Yet must I bow and obey, and deliver the will of our
   monarch;
Namely, that all your lands, and dwellings, and cattle of
   all kinds,
Forfeited be to the crown; and that you yourselves from
   this province

Be transported to other lands. God grant you may dwell
   there
Ever be faithful subjects, a happy and peaceable people!
Prisoners now I declare you; for such is his Majesty's
   pleasure!"
As, when the air is serene in the sultry solstice of
   summer,
Suddenly gathers a storm, and the deadly sling of the
   hailstones
Beats down the farmer's corn in the field and shatters
   his windows,
Hiding the sun, and strewing the ground with thatch
   from the house-roofs,
Bellowing fly the herds, and seek to break their
   enclosures;
So on the hearts of the people descended the words of
   the speaker.
Silent a moment they stood in speechless wonder, and
   then rose
Louder and ever louder a wail of sorrow and anger,
And, by one impulse moved, they madly rushed to the
   doorway.
Vain was the hope of escape; and cries and fierce
   imprecations
Rang through the house of prayer; and high o'er the
   heads of the others
Rose, with his arms uplifted, the figure of Basil the
   blacksmith,
As, on a stormy sea, a spar is tossed by the billows.
Flushed was his face and distorted with passion; and
   wildly he shouted,—
"Down with the tyrants of England! we never have
   sworn them allegiance!
Death to these foreign soldiers, who seize on our homes
   and our harvests!"
More he fain would have said, but the merciless hand of
   a soldier

Smote him upon the mouth, and dragged him down to
the pavement.

In the midst of the strife and tumult of angry
contention,
Lo! the door of the chancel opened, and Father Felician
Entered with serious mien, and ascended the steps of
the altar.
Raising his reverend hand, with a gesture he awed into
silence
All that clamorous throng; and thus he spake to his
people;
Deep were his tones and solemn in accents measured
and mournful
Spake he, as, after the tocsin's alarm, distinctly the
clock strikes.
"What is this that ye do, my children? what madness
has seized you?
Forty years of my life have I laboured among you, and
taught you,
Not in word alone, but in deed, to love one another!
Is this the fruit of my toils, of my vigils and prayers and
privations?
Have you so soon forgotten all lessons of love and
forgiveness?
This is the house of the Prince of Peace, and would you
profane it
Thus with violent deeds and hearts overflowing with
hatred?
Lo! where the crucified Christ from His cross is gazing
upon you!
See! in those sorrowful eyes what meekness and holy
compassion!
Hark! how those lips still repeat the prayer, 'O Father,
forgive them!'
Let us repeat that prayer in the hour when the wicked
assail us.

Let us repeat it now, and say, O Father, forgive them!"
Few were his words of rebuke, but deep in the hearts of
    his people
Sank they, and sobs of contrition succeeded that
    passionate outbreak,
And they repeated his prayer, and said, "O Father,
    forgive them!"

Then came the evening service. The tapers gleamed
    from the altar.
Fervent and deep was the voice of the priest, and the
    people responded,
Not with their lips alone, but their hearts; and the Ave
    Maria
Sang they, and fell on their knees, and their souls, with
    devotion translated,
Rose on the ardour of prayer, like Elijah ascending to
    heaven.

Meanwhile had spread in the village the tidings of ill,
    and on all sides
Wandered, wailing, from house to house the women
    and children.
Long at her father's door Evangeline stood, with her
    right hand
Shielding her eyes from the level rays of the sun, that,
    descending,
Lighted the village street with mysterious splendour,
    and roofed each
Peasant's cottage with golden thatch, and emblazoned
    its windows.
Long within had been spread the snow-white cloth on
    the table;
There stood the wheaten loaf, and the honey fragrant
    with wild flowers;

There stood the tankard of ale, and the cheese, fresh brought from the dairy,
And, at the head of the board, the great arm-chair of the farmer.
Thus did Evangeline wait at her father's door, as the sunset
Threw the long shadows of trees o'er the broad ambrosial meadows.
Ah! on her spirit within a deeper shadow had fallen,
And from the fields of her soul a fragrance celestial ascended,—
Charity, meekness, love, and hope, and forgiveness, and patience!
Then, all forgetful of self, she wandered into the village,
Cheering with looks and words the mournful hearts of the women,
As o'er the darkening fields with lingering steps they departed,
Urged by their household cares, and the weary feet of their children.
Down sank the great red sun, and in golden, glimmering vapours
Veiled the light of his face, like the Prophet descending from Sinai.
Sweetly over the village the bell of the Angelus sounded.

Meanwhile, amid the gloom, by the church Evangeline lingered.
All was silent within; and in vain at the door and the windows
Stood she, and listened and looked, till, overcome by emotion,
"Gabriel!" cried she aloud with tremulous voice; but no answer
Came from the graves of the dead, nor the gloomier grave of the living.

Henry Wadsworth Longfellow

The memorial church at Grand Pré National Park, Nova Scotia. Photo by Sherman Hines.

The Acadian communities that grew up around the Bay of Fundy based their agriculture on reclaimed marshland. Dykes held back the highest tides from the upper reaches of the saltmarsh and permitted the cultivation of large areas of wheat. Illustration courtesy of the Public Archives of Canada.

*When in the harvest heat she bore to the reapers
   at noontide
Flagons of home-brewed ale, ah! fair in sooth
   was the maiden*

Illustration by Frank Dicksee. From *Evangeline: the Place, the
Story, the Poem.* Cassell, Petter, Galpin & Co., New York, 1882.
In the collection of the Nova Scotia Legislative Library.

Meanwhile, apart, in the twilight gloom of a
   window's embrasure,
Sat the lovers, and whispered together,
   beholding the moonrise.

Fairest of all the maids was Evangeline,
*   Benedict's daughter!*
Noblest of all the youths was Gabriel,
*   son of the blacksmith!*

Still from the motion picture *Evangeline: A Romance of Acadia,*
circa 1920.

Vain was the hope of escape; and cries and
  fierce imprecations
Rang through the house of prayer...

Illustration by Jesse Wilcox Smith. From *Evangeline*. Houghton
Mifflin and Co., Boston, 1897. In the collection of the Nova
Scotia Legislative Library.

*Came from the neighbouring hamlets and farms
the Acadian women,
Driving in ponderous wains their household
goods to the seashore.*

Illustration by Frank Dicksee. From *Evangeline: the Place, the Story, the Poem.* Cassell, Petter, Galpin & Co., New York, 1882. In the collection of the Nova Scotia Legislative Library.

*Gabriel! be of good cheer! for if we love one
another,*
*Nothing in truth, can harm us, whatever mischances
may happen!*

*And, as a signal sound, if others like them
  peradventure
Sailed on those gloomy and midnight streams,
  blew a blast on his bugle.*

Illustration by F.O.C. Darley. From *Evangeline*. Houghton
Mifflin and Co., Boston, 1866. In the collection of the Nova
Scotia Legislative Library.

Sometimes they saw, or thought they saw, the smoke of his campfire.

Vainly he strove to rise; and Evangeline,
  kneeling beside him,
Kissed his dying lips, and laid his head
  on her bosom.

Slowly at length she returned to the tenantless house of
her father.
Smouldered the fire on the hearth, on the board was the
supper untasted,
Empty and drear was each room, and haunted with
phantoms of terror.
Sadly echoed her step on the stair and the floor of her
chamber.
In the dead of the night she heard the disconsolate rain
fall
Loud on the withered leaves of the sycamore-tree by
the window.
Keenly the lightning flashed; and the voice of the
echoing thunder
Told her that God was in heaven, and governed the
world he created!
Then she remembered the tale she had heard of the
justice of Heaven;
Soothed was her troubled soul, and she peacefully
slumbered till morning.

V

Four times the sun had risen and set; and now on the
fifth day
Cheerily called the cock to the sleeping maids of the
farm-house.
Soon o'er the yellow fields, in silent and mournful
procession,
Came from the neighbouring hamlets and farms the
Acadian women,
Driving in ponderous wains their household goods to
the sea-shore,
Pausing and looking back to gaze once more on their
dwellings,
Ere they were shut from sight by the winding road and
the woodland.

Close at their sides their children ran, and urged on the
    oxen,
While in their little hands they clasped some fragments
    of playthings.

   Thus, to the Gaspereau's mouth they hurried; and
    there on the sea-beach
Piled in confusion lay the household goods of the
    peasants.
All day long between the shore and the ships did the
    boats ply;
All day long the wains came labouring down from the
    village.
Late in the afternoon, when the sun was near to his
    setting,
Echoed far o'er the fields came the roll of drums from
    the church-yard.
Thither the women and children thronged.
    On a sudden the church doors
Opened, and forth came the guard, and marching in
    gloomy procession
Followed the long imprisoned, but patient, Acadian
    farmers.
Even as pilgrims, who journey afar from their homes
    and their country,
Sing as they go, and in singing forget they are weary
    and way-worn,
So with songs on their lips the Acadian peasants
    descended
Down from the church to the shore, amid their wives
    and their daughters.
Foremost the young men came; and, raising together
    their voices,
Sang they with tremulous lips a chant of the Catholic
    Missions:—
"Sacred heart of the Saviour! O inexhaustible fountain!
Fill our hearts this day with strength and submission
    and patience!"

Then the old men, as they marched, and the women
    that stood by the way-side,
Joined in the sacred psalm, and the birds in the
    sunshine above them
Mingled their notes therewith, like voices of spirits
    departed.

   Half-way down to the shore Evangeline waited in
    silence,
Not overcome with grief, but strong in the hour of
    affliction,—
Calmly and sadly she waited, until the procession
    approached her,
And she beheld the face of Gabriel pale with emotion.
Tears then filled her eyes, and, eagerly running to meet
    him,
Clasped she his hands, and laid her head on his
    shoulder, and whispered,—
"Gabriel! be of good cheer! for if we love one another,
Nothing, in truth, can harm us, whatever mischances
    may happen!"
Smiling she spake these words; then suddenly paused,
    for her father
Saw she slowly advancing. Alas! how changed was his
    aspect!
Gone was the glow from his cheek, and the fire from his
    eye, and his footstep
Heavier seemed with the weight of the heavy heart in
    his bosom.
But, with a smile and a sigh, she clasped his neck and
    embraced him,
Speaking words of endearment where words of comfort
    availed not.
Thus to the Gaspereau's mouth moved on that
    mournful procession.

There disorder prevailed, and the tumult and stir of
  embarking.
Busily plied the freighted boats; and in the confusion
Wives were torn from their husbands, and mothers, too
  late, saw their children
Left on the land, extending their arms, with wildest
  entreaties.
So unto separate ships were Basil and Gabriel carried,
While in despair on the shore Evangeline stood with
  her father.
Half the task was not done when the sun went down,
  and the twilight
Deepened and darkened around; and in haste the
  refluent ocean
Fled away from the shore, and left the line of the sand-
  beach
Covered with waifs of the tide, with kelp and the
  slippery sea-weed.
Farther back in the midst of the household goods and
  the wagons,
Like to a gipsy camp, or a leaguer after a battle,
All escape cut off by the sea, and the sentinels near
  them,
Lay encamped for the night the houseless Acadian
  farmers.
Back to its nethermost caves retreated the bellowing
  ocean,
Dragging adown the beach the rattling pebbles, and
  leaving
Inland and far up the shore the stranded boats of the
  sailors.
Then, as the night descended, the herds returned from
  their pastures;
Sweet was the moist still air with the odour of milk
  from their udders;
Lowing they waited, and long, at the well-known bars
  of the farm-yard,—

Waited and looked in vain for the voice and the hand of
the milkmaid.
Silence reigned in the street; from the church no
Angelus sounded,
Rose no smoke from the roofs, and gleamed no lights
from the windows.

But on the shores meanwhile the evening fires had
been kindled,
Built of the drift-wood thrown on the sands from
wrecks in the tempest.
Round them shapes of gloom and sorrowful faces were
gathered,
Voices of women were heard, and of men, and the
crying of children.
Onward from fire to fire, as from hearth to hearth in his
parish,
Wandered the faithful priest, consoling and blessing
and cheering,
Like unto shipwrecked Paul on Melita's desolate
seashore.
Thus he approached the place where Evangeline sat
with her father.
And in the flickering light beheld the face of the old
man,
Haggard and hollow and wan, and without either
thought or emotion.
E'en as the face of a clock from which the hands have
been taken.
Vainly Evangeline strove with words and caresses to
cheer him,
Vainly offered him food; yet he moved not, he looked
not, he spake not,
But, with a vacant stare, ever gazed at the flickering
fire-light.
"Benedicite!" murmured the priest, in tones of
compassion.

More he fain would have said, but his heart was full, and his accents
Faltered and paused on his lips, as the feet of a child on a threshold,
Hushed by the scene he beholds, and the awful presence of sorrow.
Silently, therefore, he laid his hand on the head of the maiden,
Raising his tearful eyes to the silent stars that above them
Moved on their way, unperturbed by the wrongs and sorrows of mortals.
Then sat he down at her side, and they wept together in silence.

Suddenly rose from the south a light, as in autumn the blood-red
Moon climbs the crystal walls of heaven, and o'er the horizon
Titan-like stretches its hundred hands upon mountain and meadow,
Seizing the rocks and the rivers, and piling huge shadows together.
Broader and ever broader it gleamed on the roofs of the village,
Gleamed on the sky and the sea, and the ships that lay in the roadstead.
Columns of shining smoke uprose, and flashes of flame were
Thrust through their folds and withdrawn like the quivering hands of a martyr.
Then as the winds seized the gleeds and the burning thatch and uplifting,
Whirled them aloft through the air, at once from a hundred housetops
Started the sheeted smoke with ashes of flame intermingled.

These things beheld in dismay the crowd on the shore
  and on shipboard.
Speechless at first they stood, then cried aloud in their
  anguish,
"We shall behold no more our homes in the village of
  Grand-Pré!"
Loud on a sudden the cocks began to crow in the farm-
  yards,
Thinking the day had dawned; and anon the lowing of
  cattle
Came on the evening breeze, by the barking of dogs
  interrupted.
Then rose the sound of dread, such as startles the
  sleeping encampments
Far in the western prairies of forests that skirt the
  Nebraska,
When the wild horses affrighted sweep by with the
  speed of the whirlwind,
Or the loud bellowing herds of buffaloes rush to the
  river.
Such was the sound that arose on the night, as the herds
  and the horses
Broke through their folds and fences, and madly rushed
  o'er the meadows.

  Overwhelmed with the sight, yet speechless, the
    priest and the maiden
Gazed on the scene of terror that reddened and widened
  before them;
And as they turned at length to speak to their silent
  companion,
Lo! from his seat he had fallen, and stretched abroad on
  the seashore
Motionless lay his form, from which the soul had
  departed.
Slowly the priest uplifted the lifeless head, and the
  maiden

Knelt at her father's side, and wailed aloud in her
    terror.
Then in a swoon she sank, and lay with her head on his
    bosom.
Through the long night she lay in deep, oblivious
    slumber;
And when she awoke from the trance, she beheld a
    multitude near her.
Faces of friends she beheld, that were mournfully
    gazing upon her;
Pallid, with tearful eyes, and looks of saddest
    compassion.
Still the blaze of the burning village illumined the
    landscape,
Reddened the sky overhead, and gleamed on the faces
    around her,
And like the day of doom it seemed to her wavering
    senses.
Then a familiar voice she heard, as it said to the
    people,—
"Let us bury him here by the sea. When a happier
    season
Brings us again to our home from the unknown land of
    our exile,
Then shall his sacred dust be piously laid in the
    churchyard."
Such were the words of the priest. And there in haste by
    the seaside,
Having the glare of the burning village for funeral
    torches,
But without bell or book, they buried the farmer of
    Grand-Pré.
And as the voice of the priest repeated the service of
    sorrow,
Lo! with a mournful sound, like the voice of a vast
    congregation,
Solemnly answered the sea, and mingled its roar with
    the dirges.

Twas the returning tide, that afar from the waste of the ocean,
With the first dawn of the day, came heaving and hurrying landward.
They recommenced once more the stir and noise of embarking;
And with the ebb of the tide the ships sailed out of the harbour,
Leaving behind them the dead on the shore, and the village in ruins.

PART THE SECOND

I

Many a weary year had passed since the burning of Grand-Pré,
When on the falling tide the freighted vessels departed,
Bearing a nation, with all its household goods, into exile,
Exile without an end, and without an example in story.
Far asunder, on separate coasts, the Acadians landed;
Scattered were they, like flakes of snow, when the wind from the north-east
Strikes aslant through the fogs that darken the Banks of Newfoundland.
Friendless, homeless, hopeless, they wandered from city to city,
From the cold lakes of the North to sultry Southern savannas,—
From the bleak shores of the sea to the lands where the Father of Waters
Seizes the hills in his hands, and drags them down to the ocean,
Deep in their sands to bury the scattered bones of the mammoth.

Friends they sought and homes; and many, despairing, heart-broken,

Asked of the earth but a grave, and no longer a friend nor a fireside.

Written their history stands on tablets of stone in the churchyards.

Long among them was seen a maiden who waited and wandered,

Lowly and meek in spirit, and patiently suffering all things.

Fair was she and young; but, alas! before her extended,

Dreary and vast and silent, the desert of life, with its pathway

Marked by the graves of those who had sorrowed and suffered before her,

Passions long extinguished, and hopes long dead and abandoned,

As the emigrant's way o'er the Western desert is marked by

Camp-fires long consumed, and bones that bleach in the sunshine.

Something there was in her life incomplete, imperfect, unfinished;

As if a morning of June, with all its music and sunshine,

Suddenly paused in the sky, and, fading, slowly descended

Into the east again, from whence it late had arisen.

Sometimes she lingered in towns, till, urged by the fever within her,

Urged by a restless longing, the hunger and thirst of the spirit,

She would commence again her endless search and endeavour;

Sometimes in churchyards strayed, and gazed on the crosses and tombstones,

Sat by some nameless grave, and thought that perhaps in its bosom

He was already at rest, and she longed to slumber
    beside him.
Sometimes a rumour, a hearsay, an inarticulate
    whisper,
Came with its airy hand to point and beckon her
    forward.
Sometimes she spake with those who had seen her
    beloved and known him,
But it was long ago, in some far-off place or forgotten.
"Gabriel Lajeunesse!" they said; "Oh yes! we have seen
    him.
He was with Basil the blacksmith, and both have gone
    to the prairies;
Coureurs-des-Bois are they, and famous hunters and
    trappers."
"Gabriel Lajeunesse!" said others; "Oh yes! we have
    seen him.
He is a Voyageur in the lowlands of Louisiana."
Then they would say,—"Dear child! why dream and
    wait for him longer?
Are there not other youths as fair as Gabriel? others
Who have hearts as tender and true, and spirits as
    loyal?
Here is Baptiste Leblanc, the notary's son, who had
    loved thee
Many a tedious year; come, give him thy hand and be
    happy!
Thou art too fair to be left to braid St. Catherine's
    tresses."
Then would Evangeline answer, serenely but sadly,—"I
    cannot!
Whither my heart has gone, there follows my hand, and
    not elsewhere.
For when the heart goes before, like a lamp, and
    illumines the pathway,
Many things are made clear, that else lie hidden in
    darkness."

Thereupon the priest, her friend and father-confessor,
Said, with a smile,—"O daughter! thy God thus
speaketh within thee!
Talk not of wasted affection, affection never was
wasted;
If it enrich not the heart of another, its waters, returning
Back to their springs, like the rain, shall fill them full of
refreshment;
That which the fountain sends forth returns again to the
fountain.
Patience; accomplish thy labor; accomplish thy work of
affection!
Sorrow and silence are strong, and patient endurance is
godlike.
Purified, strengthened, perfected, and rendered more
worthy of heaven!"
Cheered by the good man's words, Evangeline laboured
and waited.
Still in her heart she heard the funeral dirge of the
ocean,
But with its sound there was mingled a voice that
whispered, "Despair not!"
Thus did that poor soul wander in want and cheerless
discomfort,
Bleeding, barefooted, over the shards and thorns of
existence.
Let me essay, O Muse! to follow the wanderer's
footsteps;—
Not through each devious path, each changeful year of
existence,
But as a traveller follows a streamlet's course through
the valley:
Far from its margin at times, and seeing the gleam of its
water
Here and there, in some open space, and at intervals
only;
Then drawing nearer its banks, through sylvan glooms
that conceal it,

Though he behold it not, he can hear its continuous
   murmur;
Happy, at length, if he find the spot where it reaches an
   outlet.

II

It was the month of May. Far down the Beautiful River,
Past the Ohio shore and past the mouth of the Wabash,
Into the golden stream of the broad and swift
   Mississippi,
Floated a cumbrous boat, that was rowed by Acadian
   boatmen.
It was a band of exiles: a raft, as it were, from the
   shipwrecked
Nation, scattered along the coast, now floating together,
Bound by the bonds of a common belief and a common
   misfortune;
Men and women and children, who, guided by hope or
   by hearsay,
Sought for their kith and their kin among the few-acred
   farmers
On the Acadian coast, and the prairies of fair
   Opelousas.
With them Evageline went, and her guide, the Father
   Felician.
Onward o'er sunken sands, through a wilderness
   sombre with forests,
Day after day they glided adown the turbulent river;
Night after night, by their blazing fires, encamped on its
   borders.
Now through rushing chutes, among green islands,
   where plumelike
Cotton-trees nodded their shadowy crests, they swept
   with the current,
Then emerged into broad lagoons, where silvery sand-
   bars

Lay in the stream, and along the wimpling waves of
their margin,
Shining with snow-white plumes, large flocks of
pelicans waded.
Level the landscape grew, and along the shores of the
river,
Shaded by China-trees, in the midst of luxuriant
gardens,
Stood the houses of planters, with negro-cabins and
dove-cots.
They were approaching the region where reigns
perpetual summer,
Where through the Golden Coast, and groves of orange
and citron,
Sweeps with majestic curve the river away to the
eastward.
They, too, swerved from their course; and, entering the
Bayou of Plaquemine,
Soon were lost in a maze of sluggish and devious
waters,
Which, like a network of steel, extended in every
direction.
Over their heads the towering and tenebrous boughs of
the cypress
Met in a dusky arch, and trailing mosses in mid-air
Waved like banners that hang on the walls of ancient
cathedrals.
Deathlike the silence seemed, and unbroken, save by
the herons
Home to their roosts in the cedar-trees returning at
sunset,
Or by the owl, as he greeted the moon with demoniac
laughter.
Lovely the moonlight was as it glanced and gleamed on
the water,
Gleamed on the columns of cypress and cedar
sustaining the arches,

Down through whose broken vaults it fell as through
  chinks in a ruin.
Dreamlike, and indistinct, and strange were all things
  around them;
And o'er their spirits there came a feeling of wonder
  and sadness,—
Strange forebodings of ill, unseen and that cannot be
  compassed.
As, at the tramp of a horse's hoof on the turf of the
  prairies,
Far in advance are closed the leaves of the shrinking
  mimosa,
So, at the hoof-beats of fate, with sad forebodings of
  evil,
Shrinks and closes the heart, ere the stroke of doom has
  attained it.
But Evangeline's heart was sustained by a vision, that
  faintly
Floated before her eyes, and beckoned her on through
  the moonlight.
It was the thought of her brain that assumed the shape
  of a phantom.
Through those shadowy aisles had Gabriel wandered
  before her,
And every stroke of the oar now brought him nearer
  and nearer.

  Then in his place, at the prow of the boat, rose one of
    the oarsmen,
And, as a signal sound, if others like them perad-
    venture
Sailed on those gloomy and midnight streams, blew a
    blast on his bugle.
Wild through the dark colonnades and corridors leafy
    the blast rang,
Breaking the seal of silence, and giving tongues to the
    forest.

Soundless above them the banners of moss just stirred
to the music.
Multitudinous echoes awoke and died in the distance,
Over the watery floor, and beneath the reverberant
branches;
But not a voice replied; no answer came from the
darkness;
And when the echoes had ceased, like a sense of pain
was the silence.
Then Evangeline slept; but the boatmen rowed through
the midnight,
Silent at times, then singing familiar Canadian boat-
songs,
Such as they sang of old on their own Acadian river,
While through the night were heard the mysterious
sounds of the desert,
Far off,—indistinct,— as of wave or wind in the forest,
Mixed with the whoop of the crane and the roar of the
grim alligator.

Thus ere another noon they emerged from the
shades; and before them
Lay, in the golden sun, the lakes of the Atchafalaya.
Water-lilies in myriads rocked on the slight undulations
Made by the passing oars, and, resplendent in beauty,
the lotus
Lifted her golden crown above the heads of the
boatmen.
Faint was the air with the odorous breath of magnolia
blossoms,
And with the heat of noon; and numberless sylvan
islands,
Fragrant and thickly embowered with blossoming
hedges of roses,
Near to whose shores they glided along, invited to
slumber.

Soon by the fairest of these their weary oars were
    suspended.
Under the boughs of Wachita willows, that grew by the
    margin,
Safely their boat was moored; and scattered about on
    the greensward,
Tired with their midnight toil, the weary travellers
    slumbered.
Over them vast and high extended the cope of a cedar.
Swinging from its great arms, the trumpet-flower and
    the grape-vine
Hung their ladders of rope aloft like the ladder of
    Jacob,
On whose pendulous stairs the angels ascending,
    descending,
Were the swift humming-birds, that flitted from
    blossom to blossom.
Such was the vision Evangeline saw as she slumbered
    beneath it.
Filled was her heart with love, and the dawn of an
    opening heaven
Lighted her soul in sleep with the glory of regions
    celestial.

  Nearer and ever nearer, among the numberless
    islands,
Darted a light, swift boat, that sped away o'er the
    water,
Urged on its course by the sinewy arms of hunters and
    trappers.
Northward its prow was turned, to the land of the bison
    and beaver.
At the helm sat a youth, with countenance thoughtful
    and careworn.
Dark and neglected locks overshadowed his brow, and
    a sadness

Somewhat beyond his years on his face was legibly
written.
Gabriel was it, who, weary with waiting, unhappy and
restless,
All undisturbed by the dash of their oars, and of sorrow.
Swiftly they glided along, close under the lee of the
island,
But by the opposite bank, and behind a screen of
palmettos,
So that they saw not the boat, where it lay concealed in
the willows,
All undisturbed by the dash of their oars, and unseen,
were the sleepers,
Angel of God was there none to awaken the slumbering
maiden.
Swiftly they glided away, like the shade of a cloud on
the prairie.
After the sound of their oars on the tholes had died in
the distance,
As from a magic trance the sleepers awoke, and the
maiden
Said with a sigh to the friendly priest, "O Father
Felician!
Something says in my heart that near me Gabriel
wanders.
Is it a foolish dream, an idle and vague superstition?
Or has an angel passed, and revealed the truth to my
spirit?"
Then, with a blush, she added,—"Alas for my
credulous fancy!
Unto ears like thine such words as these have no
meaning."
But made answer the reverend man, and he smiled as he
answered,—
"Daughter, thy words are not idle; nor are they to me
without meaning.
Feeling is deep and still; and the word that floats on the
surface

Is as the tossing buoy, that betrays where the anchor is
hidden.
Therefore trust to thy heart, and to what the world calls
illusions.
Gabriel truly is near thee; for not far away to the
southward,
On the banks of the Têche are the towns of St. Maur
and St. Martin.
There the long-wandering bride shall be given again to
her bridegroom,
There the long-absent pastor regain his flock and his
sheepfold.
Beautiful is the land, with its prairies and forests of
fruit-trees;
Under the feet a garden of flowers, and the bluest of
heavens
Bending above, and resting its dome on the walls of the
forest.
They who dwell there have named it the Eden of
Louisiana."
With their words of cheer they arose and continued on
their journey.
Softly the evening came. The sun from the western
horizon
Like a magician extended his golden wand o'er the
landscape;
Twinkling vapours arose; and sky and water and forest
Seemed all on fire at the touch, and melted and mingled
together.
Hanging between two skies, a cloud with edges of
silver,
Floated the boat, with its dripping oars, on the
motionless water.
Filled was Evangeline's heart with inexpressible
sweetness.
Touched by the magic spell, the sacred fountains of
feeling

Glowed with the light of love, as the skies and waters
  around her.
Then from a neighbouring thicket the mockingbird,
  wildest of singers,
Swinging aloft on a willow spray that hung o'er the
  water,
Shook from his little throat such floods of delirious
  music,
That the whole air and the woods and the waves
  seemed silent to listen.
Plaintive at first were the tones and sad: then soaring to
  madness
Seemed they to follow or guide the revel of frenzied
  Bacchantes.
Single notes were then heard, in sorrowful, low
  lamentation;
Till, having gathered them all, he flung them abroad in
  derision,
As when, after a storm, a gust of wind through the tree-
  tops
Shakes down the rattling rain in a crystal shower on the
  branches.
With such a prelude as this, and hearts that throbbed
  with emotion,
Slowly they entered the Têche, where it flows through
  the green Opelousas,
And through the amber air, above the crest of the
  woodland,
Saw the column of smoke that arose from a
  neighbouring dwelling;—
Sounds of a horn they heard, and the distant lowing of
  cattle.

III

Near to the bank of the river, o're-shadowed by oaks,
  from whose branches

Garlands of Spanish moss and of mystic mistletoe
    flaunted,
Such as the Druids cut down with golden hatchets at
    Yuletide,
Stood, secluded and still, the house of the herdsman. A
    garden
Girded it round about with a belt of luxuriant blossoms,
Filling the air with fragrance. The house itself was of
    timbers
Hewn from the cypress-tree, and carefully fitted
    together.
Large and low was the roof; and on slender columns
    supported,
Rose-wreathed, vine-encircled, a broad and spacious
    veranda,
Haunt of the humming-bird and the bee, extended
    around it.
At each end of the house, amid the flowers of the
    garden,
Stationed the dove-cots were, as love's perpetual
    symbol,
Scenes of endless wooing, and endless contentions of
    rivals.
Silence reigned o'er the place. The line of shadow and
    sunshine
Ran near the tops of the trees; but the house itself was in
    shadow,
And from its chimney-top, ascending and slowly
    expanding
Into the evening air, a thin blue column of smoke rose.
In the rear of the house, from the garden gate, ran a
    pathway
Through the great groves of oak to the skirts of the
    limitless prairie,
Into whose sea of flowers the sun was slowly
    descending.
Full in his track of light, like ships with shadowy canvas

Hanging loose from their spars in a motionless calm in
the tropics,
Stood a cluster of trees, with tangled cordage of grape-
vines.

Just where the woodlands met the flowery surf of the
prairie,
Mounted upon his horse, with Spanish saddle and
stirrups,
Sat a herdsman, arrayed in gaiters and doublet of
deerskin.
Broad and brown was the face that from under the
Spanish sombrero
Gazed on the peaceful scene, with the lordly look of its
master.
Round about him were numberless herds of kine, that
were grazing
Quietly in the meadows, and breathing the vapoury
freshness
That uprose from the river, and spread itself over the
landscape.
Slowly lifting the horn that hung at his side, and
expanding
Fully his broad, deep chest, he blew a blast, that
resounded
Wildly and sweet and far, through the still damp air of
the evening.
Suddenly out of the grass the long white horns of the
cattle
Rose like flakes of foam on the adverse currents of
ocean.
Silent a moment they gazed, then bellowing rushed o'er
the prairie,
And the whole mass became a cloud, a shade in the
distance.
Then, as the herdsman turned to the house, through the
gate of the garden

Saw he the forms of the priest and the maiden
    advancing to meet him.
Suddenly down from his horse he sprang in amazement,
    and forward
Rushed with extended arms and exclamations of
    wonder;
When they beheld his face, they recognized Basil, the
    blacksmith.
Hearty his welcome was, as he led his guests to the
    garden.
There in an arbour of roses with endless question and
    answer
Gave they vent to their hearts, and renewed their
    friendly embraces.
Laughing and weeping by turns, or sitting silent and
    thoughtful.
Thoughtful, for Gabriel came not; and now dark doubts
    and misgivings
Stole o'er the maiden's heart; and Basil, somewhat
    embarrassed,
Broke the silence and said,—"If you came by the
    Atchafalaya,
How have you nowhere encountered my Gabriel's boat
    on the bayous?"
Over Evangeline's face at the words of Basil a shade
    passed.
Tears came into her eyes, and she said, with a tremulous
    accent,
"Gone? is Gabriel gone?" and, concealing her face on
    his shoulder,
All her o'erburdened heart gave way, and she wept and
    lamented.
Then the good Basil said,—and his voice grew blithe as
    he said it,—
"Be of good cheer, my child; it is only to-day he
    departed.
Foolish boy! he has left me alone with my herds and my
    horses.

71

Moody and restless grown, and tried and troubled, his
spirit
Could no longer endure the calm of this quiet existence,
Thinking ever of thee, uncertain and sorrowful ever,
Ever silent, or speaking only of thee and his troubles,
He at length had become so tedious to men and to
maidens,
Tedious even to me, that at length I bethought me, and
sent him
Unto the town of Adayes to trade for mules with the
Spaniards.
Thence he will follow the Indian trails to the Ozark
Mountains,
Hunting for furs in the forests, on rivers trapping the
beaver.
Therefore be of good cheer; we will follow the fugitive
lover;
He is not far on his way, and the Fates and the streams
are against him.
Up and away to-morrow, and through the red dew of
the morning
We will follow him fast, and bring him back to his
prison."
Then glad voices were heard, and up from the banks of
the river,
Borne aloft on his comrades' arms, came Michael the
fiddler.
Long under Basil's roof had he lived like a god on
Olympus,
Having no other care than dispensing music to mortals.
Far renowned was he for his silver locks and his fiddle.
"Long live Michael!" they cried, "our brave Acadian
minstrel!"
As they bore him aloft in triumphal procession; and
straightway
Father Felician advanced with Evangeline, greeting the
old man

Kindly and oft, and recalling the past, while Basil,
    enraptured,
Hailed with hilarious joy his old companions and
    gossips,
Laughing loud and long, and embracing mothers and
    daughters.
Much they marvelled to see the wealth of the ci-devant
    blacksmith,
All his domains and his herds, and his patriarchal
    demeanour;
Much they marvelled to hear his tales of the soil and the
    climate,
And of the prairies, whose numberless herds were his
    who would take them;
Each one thought in his heart, that he, too, would go
    and do likewise.
Thus they ascended the steps, and, crossing the breezy
    veranda,
Entered the hall of the house, where already the supper
    of Basil
Waited his late return; and they rested and feasted
    together.

Over the joyous feast the sudden darkness descended.
All was silent without, and illuming the landscape with
    silver,
Fair rose the dewy moon and the myriad stars; but
    within doors,
Brighter than these, shone the faces of friends in the
    glimmering lamplight.
Then from his station aloft, at the head of the table, the
    herdsman
Poured forth his heart and his wine together in endless
    profusion.
Lighting his pipe, that was filled with sweet
    Natchitoches tobacco,

Thus he spake to his guests, who listened, and smiled as
they listened:—
"Welcome once more, my friends, who long have been
friendless and homeless,
Welcome once more to a home, that is better perchance
than the old one!
Here no hungry winter congeals our blood like the
rivers;
Here no stony ground provokes the wrath of the farmer.
Smoothly the ploughshare runs through the soil, as a
keel through the water.
All the year round the orange-groves are in blossom;
and grass grows
More in a single night than a whole Canadian summer.
Here, too, numberless herds run wild and unclaimed in
the prairies;
Here, too, lands may be had for the asking, and forests
of timber
With a few blows of the axe are hewn and framed into
houses.
After your houses are built, and your fields are yellow
with harvests,
No King George of England shall drive you away from
your homesteads,
Burning your dwellings and barns, and stealing your
farms and your cattle."
Speaking these words, he blew a wrathful cloud from
his nostrils,
While his huge, brown hand came thundering down on
the table,
So that the guests all started; and Father Felician
astounded,
Suddenly paused, with a pinch of snuff half-way to his
nostrils.
But the brave Basil resumed, and his words were milder
and gayer:—
"Only beware of the fever, my friends, beware of the
fever!

For it is not like that of our cold Acadian climate,
Cured by wearing a spider hung round one's neck in a
nutshell!"
Then there were voices heard at the door, and footsteps
approaching
Sounded upon the stairs and the floor of the breezy
verandah.
It was the neighbouring Creoles and small Acadian
planters,
Who had been summoned all to the house of Basil the
herdsman.
Merry the meeting was of ancient comrades and
neighbours:
Friend clasped friend in his arms; and they who before
were strangers,
Meeting in exile, came straightway as friends to each
other,
Drawn by the gentle bond of a common country
together.
But in the neighbouring hall a strain of music,
proceeding
From the accordant strings of Michael's melodious
fiddle,
Broke up all further speech. Away, like children
delighted,
All things forgotten beside, they gave themselves to the
maddening
Whirl of the giddy dance, as it swept and swayed to the
music,
Dreamlike, with beaming eyes and the rush of fluttering
garments.

Meanwhile, apart at the head of the hall, the priest
and the herdsman
Sat, conversing together of past and present and future;
While Evangeline stood like one entranced, for within
her

Olden memories rose, and loud in the midst of the music

Heard she the sound of the sea, and an irrepresible sadness

Came o'er her heart, and unseen she stole forth into the garden.

Beautiful was the night. Behind the black wall of the forests,

Tipping its summit with silver, arose the moon. On the river

Fell here and there through the branches a tremulous gleam of the moonlight,

Like the sweet thoughts of love on a darkened and devious spirit.

Nearer and round about her, the manifold flowers of the garden

Poured out their souls in odours, that were their prayers and confessions

Unto the night, as it went its way, like a silent Carthusian.

Fuller of fragrance than they, and as heavy with shadows and night-dews,

Hung the heart of the maiden. The calm and the magical moonlight

Seemed to inundate her soul with indefinable longings,

As, through the garden gate, and beneath the brown shade of the oak-trees,

Passed she along the path to the edge of the measureless prairie.

Silent it lay, with a silvery haze upon it, and fireflies

Gleamed and floated away in mingled and infinite numbers.

Over her head the stars, the thoughts of God in the heavens,

Shone on the eyes of man, who had ceased to marvel and worship,

Save when a blazing comet was seen on the walls of that temple,

As if a hand had appeared and written upon them,
  "Upharsin."
And the soul of the maiden, between the stars and the
  fire-flies,
Wandered alone, and she cried,—"O Gabriel! O my
  beloved!
Art thou so near unto me, and yet I cannot behold thee?
Art thou so near unto me, and yet thy voice does not
  reach me?
Ah! how often thy feet have trod this path to the
  prairie!
Ah! how often thine eyes have looked on the
  woodlands around me!
Ah! how often beneath this oak, returning from labour,
Thou hast lain down to rest, and to dream of me in thy
  slumbers!
When shall these eyes behold, these arms be folded
  about thee?"
Loud and sudden and near the notes of a whippoorwill
  sounded
Like a flute in the woods; and anon, through the
  neighbouring thickets,
Farther and farther away it floated and dropped into
  silence.
"Patience!" whispered the oaks from oracular caverns
  of darkness:
And, from the moonlit meadow, a sigh responded, "To-
  morrow!"

  Bright rose the sun next day; and all the flowers of
    the garden
Bathed his shining feet with their tears, and anointed his
  tresses
With the delicious balm that they bore in their vases of
  crystal.
"Farewell!" said the priest, as he stood at the shadowy
  threshold;

"See that you bring us the Prodigal Son from his fasting
and famine;
And, too, the Foolish Virgin, who slept when the
bridegroom was coming."
"Farewell!" answered the maiden, and, smiling, with
Basil descended
Down to the river's brink, where the boatmen already
were waiting.
Thus beginning their journey with morning, and
sunshine, and gladness,
Swiftly they followed the flight of him who was
speeding before them,
Blown by the blast of fate like a dead leaf over the
desert.
Not that day, nor the next, nor yet the day that
succeeded,
Found they the trace of his course, in lake or forest or
river,
Nor, after many days, had they found him; but vague
and uncertain
Rumours alone were their guides through a wild and
desolate country;
Till, at the little inn of the Spanish town of Adayes,
Weary and worn, they alighted, and learned from the
garrulous landlord,
That on the day before, with horses and guides and
companions,
Gabriel left the village, and took the road of the
prairies.

IV

Far in the West there lies a desert land, where the
mountains
Lift, through perpetual snows, their lofty and luminous
summits.

Down from their jagged, deep ravines, where the gorge, like a gateway,
Opens a passage rude to the wheels of the emigrant's wagon,
Westward the Oregon flows and the Walleway and Owyhee.
Eastward, with devious course, among the Windriver mountains,
Through the Sweet-water Valley precipitate leaps the Nebraska;
And to the south, from Fontaine-qui-bout and the Spanish sierras,
Fretted with sands and rocks, and swept by the wind of the desert,
Numberless torrents, with ceaseless sound, descend to the ocean,
Like the great chords of a harp, in loud and solemn vibrations.
Spreading between these streams are the wondrous, beautiful prairies;
Billowy bays of grass ever rolling in shadow and sunshine,
Bright with luxuriant clusters of roses and purple amorphas.
Over them wandered the buffalo herds, and the elk and the roebuck;
Over them wandered the wolves, and herds of riderless horses;
Fires that blast and blight, and winds that are weary with travel;
Over them wander the scattered tribes of Ishmael's children,
Staining the desert with blood; and above their terrible war-trails
Circles and sails aloft, on pinions majestic, the vulture,
Like the implacable soul of a chieftain slaughtered in battle,

By invisible stairs ascending and scaling the heavens.
Here and there rise smokes from the camps of these
savage marauders;
Here and there rise groves from the margins of swift-
running rivers;
And the grim, taciturn bear, the anchorite monk of the
desert,
Climbs down their dark ravines to dig for roots by the
brookside;
And over all is the sky, the clear and crystalline heaven,
Like the protecting hand of God inverted above them.

Into this wonderful land, at the base of the Ozark
Mountains,
Gabriel far had entered, with hunters and trappers
behind him.
Day after day, with their Indian guides, the maiden and
Basil
Followed his flying steps, and thought each day to
o'ertake him.
Sometimes they saw, or thought they saw, the smoke of
his camp-fire
Rise in the morning air from the distant plain; but at
nightfall,
When they had reached the place, they found only
embers and ashes.
And, though their hearts were sad at times and their
bodies were weary,
Hope still guided them on, as the magic Fata Morgana
Showed them her lakes of light, that retreated and
vanished before them.

Once, as they sat by their evening fire, there silently
entered
Into their little camp an Indian woman, whose features

Wore deep traces of sorrow, and patience as great as her
    sorrow.
She was a Shawnee woman returning home to her
    people,
From the far-off hunting grounds of the cruel
    Camanches,
Where her Canadian husband, a Coureur-de-Bois, had
    been murdered.
Touched were their hearts at her story, and warmest
    and friendliest welcome
Gave they, with words of cheer, and she sat and feasted
    among them
On the buffalo meat and the venison cooked on the
    embers.
But when their meal was done, and Basil and all his
    companions,
Worn with the long day's march and the chase of the
    deer and the bison,
Stretched themselves on the ground, and slept where
    the quivering fire-light
Flashed on their swarthy cheeks, and their forms
    wrapped up in their blankets,
Then at the door of Evangeline's tent she sat and
    repeated
Slowly, with soft, low voice, and the charm of her
    Indian accent,
All the tale of her love, with its pleasures, and pains,
    and reverses.
Much Evangeline wept at the tale, and to know that
    another
Hapless heart like her own had loved and had been
    disappointed.
Moved to the depths of her soul by pity and woman's
    compassion,
Yet in her sorrow pleased that one who had suffered
    was near her,
She in turn related her love and all its disasters.

Mute with wonder the Shawnee sat, and when she had
    ended
Still was mute; but at length, as if a mysterious horror
Passed through her brain, she spake, and repeated the
    tale of the Mowis;
Mowis, he bridegroom of snow, who won and wedded
    a maiden,
But, when the morning came, arose and passed from the
    wigwam,
Fading and melting away and dissolving into the
    sunshine,
Till she beheld him no more, though she followed far
    into the forest.
Then, in those sweet, low tones, that seemed like a
    weird incantation,
Told she the tale of the fair Lilinau, who was wooed by
    a phantom,
That, through the pines, o'er her father's lodge, in the
    hush of the twilight,
Breathed like the evening wind, and whispered love to
    the maiden,
Till she followed his green and waving plume through
    the forest,
And nevermore returned, nor was seen again by her
    people.
Silent with wonder and strange surprise, Evangeline
    listened
To the soft flow of her magical words, till the region
    around her
Seemed like enchanted ground, and her swarthy guest
    the enchantress.
Slowly over the tops of the Ozark Mountains the moon
    rose,
Lighting the little tent, and with a mysterious splendour
Touching the sombre leaves, and embracing and filling
    the woodland.
With a delicate sound the brook rushed by, and the
    branches.

Swayed and sighed overhead in scarcely audible
  whispers.
Filled with the thoughts of love was Evangeline's heart,
  but a secret,
Subtle sense crept in of pain and indefinte terror,
As the cold poisonous snake creeps into the nest of the
  swallow.
It was no earthly fear. A breath from the region of
  spirits
Seemed to float in the air of night; and she felt for a
  moment
That, like the Indian maid, she, too, was pursuing a
  phantom.
With this thought she slept, and the fear and the
  phantom had vanished.

  Early upon the morrow the march was resumed; and
  the Shawnee
Said, as they journeyed along,—"On the western slope
  of these mountains
Dwells in his little village the Black Robe chief of the
  Mission.
Much he teaches the people, and tells them of Mary and
  Jesus;
Loud laugh their hearts with joy, and weep with pain,
  as they hear him."
Then, with a sudden and secret emotion, Evangeline
  answered,—
"Let us go to the Mission, for there good tidings await
  us!"
Thither they turned their steeds; and behind a spur of
  the mountains,
Just as the sun went down, they heard a murmur of
  voices,
And in a meadow green and broad, by the bank of a
  river,

Saw the tents of the Christians, the tents of the Jesuit
Mission.

Under a towering oak, that stood in the midst of the
village,

Knelt the Black Robe chief with his children. A crucifix
fastened

High on the trunk of the tree, and over-shadowed by
grape-vines,

Looked with its agonised face on the multitude kneeling
beneath it.

This was their rural chapel. Aloft, through the intricate
arches

Of its aerial roof, arose the chant of their vespers,

Mingling its notes with the soft susurrus and sighs of the
branches.

Silent, with heads uncovered, the travellers, nearer
approaching,

Knelt on the swarded floor, and joined in the evening
devotions.

But when the service was done, and the benediction had
fallen

Forth from the hands of the priest, like seed from the
hands of the sower,

Slowly the reverend man advanced to the strangers, and
bade them

Welcome; and when they replied, he smiled with
benignant expression,

Hearing the homelike sounds of his mother-tongue in
the forest,

And, with words of kindness, conducted them into his
wigwam.

There upon mats and skins they reposed, and on cakes
of the maize-ear

Feasted, and slaked their thirst from the water-gourd of
the teacher.

Soon was their story told; and the priest with solemnity
answered:—

"Not six suns have risen and set since Gabriel, seated
On this mat by my side, where now the maiden reposes,
Told me this same sad tale; then arose and continued his
   journey!"
Soft was the voice of the priest, and he spake with an
   accent of kindness;
But on Evangeline's heart fell his words as in winter the
   snow-flakes
Fall into some lone nest from which the birds have
   departed.
"Far to the north he has gone," continued the priest;
   "but in autumn,
When the chase is done, will return again to the
   Mission."
Then Evangeline said, and her voice was meek and
   submissive,
"Let me remain with thee, for my soul is sad and
   afflicted."
So seemed it wise and well unto all; and betimes on the
   morrow,
Mounting his Mexican steed, with his Indian guides and
   companions,
Homeward Basil returned, and Evangeline stayed at the
   Mission.

   Slowly, slowly, slowly the days succeeded each
   other,—
Days and weeks and months; and the fields of maize
   that were springing
Green from the ground when a stranger she came, now
   waving above her,
Lifted their slender shafts, with leaves interlacing, and
   forming
Cloisters for mendicant crows and granaries pillaged by
   squirrels.
Then in the golden weather the maize was husked, and
   the maidens

Blushed at each blood-red ear, for that betokened a
    lover,
But at the crooked laughed, and called it a thief in the
    corn-field.
Even the blood-red ear to Evangeline brought not her
    lover.
"Patience!" the priest would say; "Have faith, and thy
    prayer will be answered!
Look at this vigorous plant that lifts its head from the
    meadow,
See how its leaves are turned to the north, as true as the
    magnet;
This is the compass flower, that the finger of God has
    planted
Here in the houseless wild, to direct the traveller's
    journey
Over the sea-like, pathless, limitless waste of the desert.
Such in the soul of man is faith. The blossoms of
    passion,
Gay and luxuriant flowers, are brighter and fuller of
    fragrance,
But they beguile us, and lead us astray, and their odour
    is deadly.
Only this humble plant can guide us here, and hereafter
Crown us with asphodel flowers, that are wet with the
    dews of nepenthe."

So came the autumn, and passed, and the winter,—
    yet Gabriel came not;
Blossomed the opening spring, and the notes of the
    robin and blue-bird
Sounded sweet upon wold and in wood, yet Gabriel
    came not.
But on the breath of the summer winds a rumor was
    wafted
Sweeter than song of bird, or hue or odour of blossom.

Far to the north and east, it said, in the Michigan
   forests,
Gabriel had his lodge by the banks of the Saginaw
   River.
And, with returning guides, that sought the lakes of St.
   Lawrence,
Saying a sad farewell, Evangeline went from the
   Mission.
When over weary ways, by long and perilous marches,
She had attained at length the depths of the Michigan
   forests,
Found she the hunter's lodge deserted and fallen to
   ruin!

   Thus did the long sad years glide on, and in seasons
      and places
Divers and distant far was seen the wandering
   maiden;—
Now in the Tents of Grace of the meek Moravian
   Missions,
Now in the noisy camps and the battlefields of the
   army,
Now in secluded hamlets, in towns and populous cities.
Like a phantom she came, and passed away
   unremembered.
Fair was she and young, when in hope began the long
   journey;
Faded was she and old, when in disappointment it
   ended.
Each succeeding year stole something away from her
   beauty,
Leaving behind it, broader and deeper, the gloom and
   the shadow.
Then there appeared and spread faint streaks of gray
   o'er her forehead,
Dawn of another life, that broke o'er her earthly
   horizon,

As in the eastern sky the first faint streaks of the
morning.

V

In that delightful land which is washed by the Delaware
waters,
Guarding in sylvan shades the name of Penn the
apostle,
Stands on the banks of its beautiful stream the city he
founded.
There all the air is balm, and the peach is the emblem of
beauty,
And the streets still re-echo the names of the trees of the
forest,
As if they fain would appease the Dryads whose haunts
they molested.
There from the troubled sea had Evangeline landed, an
exile,
Finding among the children of Penn a home and a
country.
There old René Leblanc had died; and when he
departed,
Saw at his side only one of all his hundred descendants.
Something at least there was in the friendly streets of
the city,
Something that spake to her heart, and made her no
longer a stranger;
And her ear was pleased with the Thee and Thou of the
Quakers,
For it recalled the past, the old Acadian country,
Where all men were equal, and all were brothers and
sisters.
So, when the fruitless search, the disappointed
endeavour,
Ended, to recommence no more upon earth,
uncomplaining,

Thither, as leaves the light, were turned her thoughts
and her footsteps.
As from a mountain's top the rainy mists of the
morning
Roll away, and afar we behold the landscape below us,
Sun-illumined, with shining rivers and cities and
hamlets,
So fell the mists from her mind, and she saw the world
far below her,
Dark no longer, but illumined with love; and the
pathway
Which she had climbed so far, lying smooth and fair in
the distance,
Gabriel was not forgotten. Within her heart was his
image,
Clothed in the beauty of love and youth, as last she
beheld him,
Only more beautiful made by his deathlike silence and
absence.
Into her thoughts of him time entered not, for it was
not.
Over him years had no power; he was not changed, but
transfigured;
He had become to her heart as one who is dead, and not
absent;
Patience and abnegation of self, and devotion to others,
This was the lesson a life of trial and sorrow had taught
her.
So was her love diffused, but, like to some odorous
spices,
Suffered no waste nor loss, though filling the air with
aroma.
Other hope had she none, nor wish in life, but to follow
Meekly, with reverent steps, the sacred feet of her
Saviour.
Thus many years she lived as a Sister of Mercy;
frequenting

Lonely and wretched roofs in the crowded lanes of the
  city,
Where distress and want concealed themselves from the
  sunlight,
Where disease and sorrow in garrets languished
  neglected.
Night after night, when the world was asleep, as the
  watchman repeated
Loud, through the gusty streets, that all was well in the
  city,
High at some lonely window he saw the light of her
  taper.
Day after day, in the gray of the dawn, as slow through
  the suburbs
Plodded the German farmer, with flowers and fruits for
  the market,
Met he that meek, pale face, returning home from its
  watchings.

  Then it came to pass that a pestilence fell on the city,
Presaged by wondrous signs, and mostly by flocks of
  wild pigeons,
Darkening the sun in their flight, with naught in their
  craws but an acorn.
And, as the tides of the sea arise in the mouth of
  September,
Flooding some silver stream, till it spreads to a lake in
  the meadow,
So death flooded life, and o'erflowing its natural
  margin,
Spread to a brackish lake, the silver stream of existence.
Wealth had no power to bribe, nor beauty to charm, the
  oppressor;
But all perished alike beneath the scourge of his
  anger;—
Only, alas! the poor, who had neither friends nor
  attendants,

Crept away to die in the almshouse, home of the
    homeless.
Then in the suburbs it stood, in the midst of meadows
    and woodlands;—
Now the city surrounds it; but still, with its gateway and
    wicket
Meek, in the midst of splendour, its humble walls seem
    to echo
Softly the words of the Lord:—"The poor ye always
    have with you."
Thither, by night and by day, came the Sister of Mercy.
    The dying
Looked up into her face, and thought, indeed, to behold
    there
Gleams of celestial light encircle her forehead with
    splendour,
Such as the artist paints o'er the brows of saints and
    apostles,
Or such as hangs by night o'er a city seen at a distance.
Unto their eyes it seemed the lamps of the city celestial,
Into whose shining gates ere long their spirits would
    enter.

   Thus, on a Sabbath morn, through the streets,
    deserted and silent,
Wending her quiet way, she entered the door of the
    almshouse.
Sweet on the summer air was the odour of flowers in
    the garden;
And she paused on her way to gather the fairest among
    them,
That the dying once more might rejoice in their
    fragrance and beauty.
Then, as she mounted the stairs to the corridors, cooled
    by the east-wind,

Distant and soft on her ear fell the chimes from the
   belfry of Christ Church,
While, intermingled with these, across the meadows
   were wafted
Sounds of psalms, that were sung by the Swedes in their
   church at Wicaco.
Soft as descending wings fell the calm of the hour on
   her spirit:
Something within her said,—"At length thy trials are
   ended;"
And, with light in her looks, she entered the chambers
   of sickness.
Noiselessly moved about the assiduous careful
   attendants,
Moistening the feverish lip, and the aching brow, and in
   silence
Closing the sightless eyes of the dead, and concealing
   their faces,
Where on their pallets they lay, like drifts of snow by
   the roadside.
Many a languid head, upraised as Evangeline entered,
Turned on its pillow of pain to gaze while she passed,
   for her presence
Fell on their hearts like a ray of the sun on the walls of a
   prison.
And, as she looked around, she saw how Death, the
   consoler,
Laying his hand upon many a heart, had healed it for
   ever.
Many familiar forms had disappeared in the night time;
Vacant their places were, or filled already by strangers.

   Suddenly, as if arrested by fear or a feeling of
      wonder,
Still she stood, with her colourless lips apart, while a
   shudder

Ran through her frame, and, forgotten, the flowerets
    dropped from her fingers,
And from her eyes and cheeks the light and bloom of
    the morning.
Then there escaped from her lips a cry of such terrible
    anguish,
That the dying heard it, and started up from their
    pillows.
On the pallet before her was stretched the form of an
    old man.
Long, and thin, and gray were the locks that shaded his
    temples;
But, as he lay in the morning light, his face for a
    moment
Seemed to assume once more the forms of its earlier
    manhood;
So are wont to be changed the faces of those who are
    dying.
Hot and red on his lips still burned the flush of the
    fever,
As if life, like the Hebrew, with blood had besprinkled
    its portals,
That the Angel of Death might see the sign, and pass
    over.
Motionless, senseless, dying, he lay, and his spirit
    exhausted
Seemed to be sinking down through infinite depths in
    the darkness,
Darkness of slumber and death, forever sinking and
    sinking.
Then through those realms of shade, in multiplied
    reverberations,
Heard he that cry of pain, and through the hush that
    succeeded
Whispered a gentle voice, in accents tender and saint-
    like,
"Gabriel! O my beloved!" and died away into silence.

Then he beheld, in a dream, once more the home of his
 childhood;
Green Acadian meadows, with sylvan rivers among
 them,
Village, and mountain, and woodlands; and, walking
 under their shadow,
As in the days of her youth, Evangeline rose in his
 vision.
Tears came into his eyes; and as slowly he lifted his
 eyelids,
Vanished the vision away, but Evangeline knelt by his
 bedside.
Vainly he strove to whisper her name, for the accents
 unuttered
Died on his lips, and their motion revealed what his
 tongue would have spoken.
Vainly he strove to rise; and Evangeline, kneeling
 beside him,
Kissed his dying lips, and laid his head on her bosom.
Sweet was the light of his eyes; but it suddenly sank into
 darkness,
As when a lamp is blown out by a gust of wind at a
 casement.

  All was ended now, the hope, and the fear, and the
 sorrow,
All the aching of heart, the restless, unsatisfied longing,
All the dull, deep pain, and constant anguish of
 patience!
And, as she pressed once more the lifeless head to her
 bosom,
Meekly she bowed her own, and muttered, "Father, I
 thank Thee!"

  Still stands the forests primeval; but far away from its
 shadow,

Side by side, in their nameless graves, the lovers are sleeping.
Under the humble walls of the little Catholic church yard,
In the heart of the city, they lie, unknown and unnoticed.
Daily the tides of life go ebbing and flowing beside them,
Thousands of throbbing hearts, where theirs are at rest and forever,
Thousands of aching brains, where theirs no longer are busy,
Thousands of toiling hands, where theirs have ceased from their labours,
Thousands of weary feet, where theirs have completed their journey!

Still stands the forest primeval; but under the shade of its branches
Dwells another race, with other customs and language.
Only along the shore of the mournful and misty Atlantic
Linger a few Acadian peasants, whose fathers from exile
Wandered back to their native land to die in its bosom.
In the fisherman's cot the wheel and the loom are still busy;
Maidens still wear their Norman caps and their kirtles of homespun,
And by the evening fire repeat Evangeline's story,
While from its rocky caverns the deep-voiced, neighbouring ocean
Speaks, and in accents disconsolate answers the wail of the forest.